A Beginning-to-Read Book

St. Patrick's Day

by Mary Lindeen

NORWOOD HOUSE PRESS

DEAR CAREGIVER, The *Beginning to Read—Read and Discover* books provide emergent readers the opportunity to explore the world through nonfiction while building early reading skills. The text integrates both common sight words and content vocabulary. These key words are featured on lists provided at the back of the book to help your child expand his or her sight word recognition, which helps build reading fluency. The content words expand vocabulary and support comprehension.

Nonfiction text is any text that is factual. The Common Core State Standards call for an increase in the amount of informational text reading among students. The Standards aim to promote college and career readiness among students. Preparation for college and career endeavors requires proficiency in reading complex informational texts in a variety of content areas. You can help your child build a foundation by introducing nonfiction early. To further support the CCSS, you will find Reading Reinforcement activities at the back of the book that are aligned to these Standards.

Above all, the most important part of the reading experience is to have fun and enjoy it!

Sincerely,

Shannon Cannon

Shannon Cannon, Ph.D.
Literacy Consultant

Norwood House Press • P.O. Box 316598 • Chicago, Illinois 60631
For more information about Norwood House Press please visit our website at
www.norwoodhousepress.com or call 866-565-2900.
© 2016 Norwood House Press. Beginning-to-Read™ is a trademark of Norwood House Press.
All rights reserved. No part of this book may be reproduced or utilized in any form or by any
means without written permission from the publisher.

Editor: Judy Kentor Schmauss
Designer: Lindaanne Donohoe

Photo Credits:

Shutterstock, cover, 1, 3, 4-5, 6-7, 8 (©EPG_EuroPhotoGraphics), 9 (©Stuart Monk), 10-11, 12-13, 20-21 (©meunierd), 22 (©Stuart Monk), 23 (©Valentyna Chukhlyebov), 24-25; Dreamstime, 14-15, 16-17 (©Deborah Hewitt), 18-19 (©Ken Pilon); iStock, 28-29; Phil Martin, 26-27

Library of Congress Cataloging-in-Publication Data
Lindeen, Mary.
St. Patrick's day / by Mary Lindeen.
pages cm. – (A beginning to read book)
Summary: "Learn about St. Patrick's Day traditions and symbols, including shamrocks, wearing green, eating corned beef and cabbage, the story of St. Patrick, leprechauns, and more. This title includes reading activities and a word list"– Provided by publisher.
ISBN 978-1-59953-687-3 (library edition : alk. paper)
ISBN 978-1-60357-772-4 (ebook)
1. Saint Patrick's Day–Juvenile literature. I. Title.
GT4995.P3L56 2015
394.262–dc23
2014047627

Manufactured in the United States of America in Stevens Point, Wisconsin. 275N–062015

St. Patrick's Day is a special
day in March.
It is always on the same date.

People decorate for St. Patrick's Day.

They use green shamrocks.

Shamrocks have three leaves.

People think they bring good luck.

People wear green on St. Patrick's Day.

They have parades, too.

Look!

This river is even made green.

DuSable Bridge

Some people have special food on St. Patrick's Day.

They have corned beef and cabbage.

St. Patrick's Day
comes from Ireland.

Ireland is in Europe.

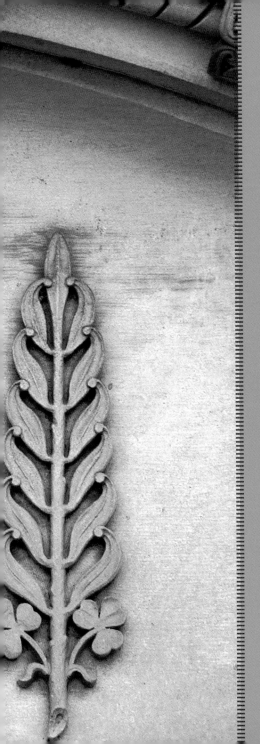

St. Patrick was a real man in Ireland.

He lived there a long time ago.

Some say there were many snakes in Ireland.

St. Patrick made all of them go away.

That is why a day
is named after him.

This man looks like a leprechaun.

Stories about leprechauns
also come from Ireland.

Some stories say
that leprechauns
hide pots of gold.

Some say the gold
is at the end of a
rainbow.

Others say a leprechaun will give you his gold.

But you have to catch him first!

Happy St. Patrick's Day!